EXPLORING EARTH

By Mary Austen

Published in 2018 by
KidHaven Publishing, an Imprint of Greenhaven Publishing, LLC
353 3rd Avenue
Suite 255
New York, NY 10010

Designer: Deanna Paternostro
Editor: Vanessa Oswald

Photo credits: Cover (Earth), p. 11 MarcelClemens/Shutterstock.com; cover (background), back cover, pp. 9, 15 (background), 21 (background) Vadim Sadovski/Shutterstock.com; p. 5 xtock/ Shutterstock.com; pp. 6–7 Christos Georghiou/Shutterstock.com; p. 13 Radu Bercan/ Shutterstock.com; p. 15 (top left) ESB Professional/Shutterstock.com; p. 15 (top right) Iakov Kalinin/ Shutterstock.com; p. 15 (bottom left) Perfect Lazybones/Shutterstock.com; p. 15 (bottom center) Dmitry Polonskiy/Shutterstock.com; p. 15 (bottom right) Galyna Andrushko/Shutterstock.com; p. 17 Lukiyanova Natalia frenta/Shutterstock.com; p. 19 Adwo/Shutterstock.com; p. 21 (top) Fotos593/ Shutterstock.com; p. 21 (bottom) isoga/Shutterstock.com.

Cataloging-in-Publication Data

Names: Austen, Mary.
Title: Exploring earth / Mary Austen.
Description: New York : KidHaven Publishing, 2018. | Series: Journey through our solar system | Includes index.
Identifiers: ISBN 9781534522855 (pbk.) | 9781534522749 (library bound) | ISBN 9781534522473 (6 pack) | ISBN 9781534522695 (ebook)
Subjects: LCSH: Earth (Planet)–Juvenile literature.
Classification: LCC QB631.4 A97 2018 | DDC 525–dc23

Printed in the United States of America

CPSIA compliance information: Batch #BS17KL: For further information contact Greenhaven Publishing LLC, New York, New York at 1-844-317-7404.

Please visit our website, www.greenhavenpublishing.com. For a free color catalog of all our high-quality books, call toll free 1-844-317-7404 or fax 1-844-317-7405.

CONTENTS

EARTH IS HOME

Earth is the planet we live on. It's the third planet from the sun. Our planet is the only one in the **solar system** known to have living things, including people, animals, and plants.

Scientists believe Earth
is 4.5 billion years old!

Earth is made up of air, water, and land. When people look at Earth from space, it may look blue. This is because most of Earth is made up of water.

Earth

Parts also may look green and brown, which is the color of the land. The swirls of white are clouds.

Earth is the fifth largest planet in the solar system.

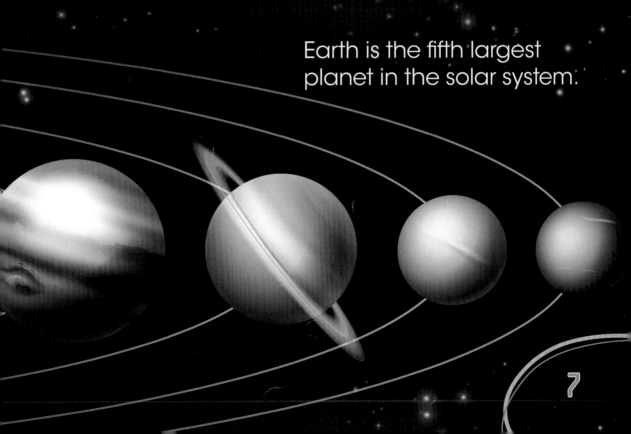

EARTH SPINS!

Like all the other planets, Earth **orbits** the sun. It takes Earth about 365 days, or 1 year, to fully orbit the sun. Earth also spins around once every 24 hours, which is the length of a day.

Because Earth is tilted on its **axis**, the most northern and southern parts of the planet may have 24 hours of daylight or darkness depending on the time of year.

sun

9

THE MOON

Earth has 1 moon that orbits the planet every 28 days. As the moon orbits Earth, it looks as if it changes shape at different points.

Scientists know more about the surface of the moon than they know about the bottom of the oceans.

moon

EARTH'S AIR

The air on Earth is special. Earth's air helps make weather. People, animals, and plants also need to take in Earth's air to live.

Earth's air helps keep the planet safe from dangerous objects such as **meteors**.

13

EARTH'S CRUST

Another name for Earth's ground is its crust. The crust can look like plains, mountains, deserts, forests, oceans, and many other landforms.

How many of Earth's landforms have you seen?

ocean

forest

mountains

desert

plains

15

Earth's crust is the thinnest of its three main **layers**. The other layers are the mantle and the core. Earth's mantle is the layer underneath the crust and is made of soft, hot rock. The core is the center layer and is made of **metal**.

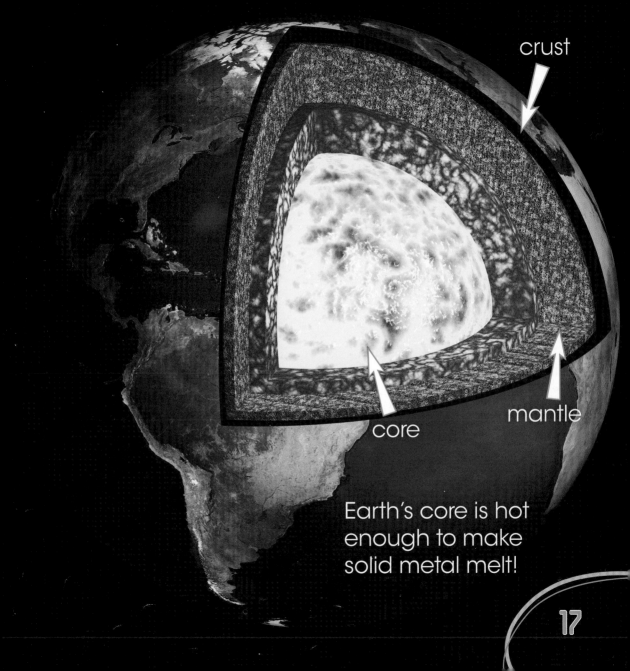

crust

mantle

core

Earth's core is hot enough to make solid metal melt!

People use Earth's crust for many different things. Small towns and large cities are built on it, and crops are grown on Earth's crust. Metal and oil are also taken from the crust.

Scientists learn more about the layers of the crust by drilling into the earth.

crust

drill

EARTH'S CRUST MOVES!

Earth's crust moves too slowly for the human eye to see on a daily basis. A change in Earth's crust is often seen only after many years go by. Changes in Earth's crust can also cause **earthquakes** and **volcanoes!**

volcano

earthquake

Earth is an amazing planet, and we get to live on it!

GLOSSARY

axis: An imaginary line that Earth is tilted on and rotates around.

earthquake: The shaking of the ground caused by the movement of Earth's crust.

layer: One part of something lying over or under another.

metal: A shiny rock, such as iron or gold, found in Earth's layers.

meteor: A chunk of rock or metal from space that falls through Earth's atmosphere, also called a "shooting star."

orbit: To travel in a circle or oval around something.

solar system: The sun and all the space objects that orbit it, including the planets and their moons.

volcano: An opening in a planet's surface through which hot, liquid rock sometimes flows.

FOR MORE INFORMATION

Websites

NASA: Earth
www.nasa.gov/topics/earth/index.html
NASA provides news about and pictures of Earth.

National Geographic Kids: Mission to Earth
kids.nationalgeographic.com/explore/space/
mission-to-earth/#earth-planet.jpg
This website features useful facts about Earth.

Books

Bloom, J. P. *Earth*. Minneapolis, MN: Abdo Kids, 2015.

Harman, Alice. *Earth*. New York, NY: Windmill Books, 2016.

York, Penelope. *Earth*. New York, NY: DK Publishing, 2015.

INDEX